Understanding Binary Numbers

Concepts in Computer Systems (Volume 1)

Eric Sakk, Ph.D.

Preface

This book is directed toward readers seeking a concise introduction to binary numbers with an inclination toward understanding computer systems. The material presented can be used as a supplement for courses relevant to computer science and computer engineering anywhere from the high school level up to the college level. Several in-chapter and end-of-chapter exercises are included in order to ensure the interested reader is able to practice and fully internalize the topics presented. Depending upon the level of the reader and the rate at which the material is covered, the book topics can be mastered within a period of two to six weeks.

Table of Contents

Chapter One: Powers of Two

Understanding binary numbers in the context of computer systems requires knowing and internalizing successive integer powers of two. It is crucial, at the minimum, to memorize powers of two from $2^0 = 1$ up to $2^{19} = 524288$. After that, we shall see that a very natural pattern begins to arise making it a straightforward exercise to generate successive powers of two.

n	2^n	=	n	2^n	=	Terminology
0	2^0	1	10	2^{10}	1024	1K
1	2^1	2	11	2^{11}	2048	2K
2	2^2	4	12	2^{12}	4096	4K
3	2^3	8	13	2^{13}	8192	8K
4	2^4	16	14	2^{14}	16384	16K
5	2^5	32	15	2^{15}	32768	32K
6	2^6	64	16	2^{16}	65536	64K
7	2^7	128	17	2^{17}	131072	128K
8	2^8	256	18	2^{18}	262144	256K
9	2^9	512	19	2^{19}	524288	512K

Table 1.1: Nonnegative powers of 2 up to 512K

Table 1.1 lists all successive integer powers of two from 2^0 up to 2^{19}. When the boundary is crossed from $2^9 = 512$ to $2^{10} = 1024$, it becomes convenient to introduce some shorthand notation that reduces the need to write out the whole number. Classically, the word 'kilo' (abbreviated by the letter 'k') is a prefix reserved for multiplying a value by $10^3 = 1000$.

Although, for powers of two, this analogy is not perfect, the use of the 'K' notation is close enough and quite useful for approximating powers of two. Clearly, $1000 \neq 1024$ and $64000 \neq 65536$; but, when this analogy is applied, one can easily observe a repeatable pattern between powers of two from $n = 0$ to $n = 9$ and powers of two from $n = 10$ to $n = 19$. This pattern is easily explainable based upon the rules for exponents. If one chooses any value of 'i' between i=0 and i=9, it should be clear that $2^{(10+i)} = 2^{10}2^i = (1024)2^i = (1K) 2^i$. So, for example, setting i=8 yields $2^{18} = 2^{(10+8)} = 2^8(1K) = 256K$ as can be seen in the above table.

This approximation can be further extended in order to abbreviate higher powers of two. Table 1.2 shows the classical definitions of prefixes such as 'mega', 'giga' and 'tera' expressed as powers of ten.

Prefix	Abbreviation	Multiplier
Kilo	K	10^3
Mega	M	10^6
Giga	G	10^9
Tera	T	10^{12}
Peta	P	10^{15}
Exa	E	10^{18}

Table 1.2: Classical prefix abbreviations for powers of ten

Oftentimes, these prefixes are used in conjunction with computer systems terminology such as **'bit'** or **'byte'** (which will be defined in the following chapters). For example, kilobyte (1KB=1024 bytes), megabyte (MB), gigabyte (GB), terabyte (TB) and petabyte (PB) are terms commonly used to define measures of system storage capacity. (As a side note, engineering and physical sciences usually use a lower case 'k' for kilo, but the computer systems community appears to have partially disregarded this convention. No worries – both 'kB' and 'KB' appear to be acceptable at this point - just as long as everyone understands what everyone means.)

Applying the set of prefixes listed in Table 1.3, it is a straightforward exercise to continue on to higher powers of two as listed in Table 1.3.

n	2^n	=	n	2^n	=	n	2^n	=
20	2^{20}	1M	30	2^{30}	1G	40	2^{40}	1T
21	2^{21}	2M	31	2^{31}	2G	41	2^{41}	2T
22	2^{22}	4M	32	2^{32}	4G	42	2^{42}	4T
23	2^{23}	8M	33	2^{33}	8G	43	2^{43}	8T
24	2^{24}	16M	34	2^{34}	16G	44	2^{44}	16T
25	2^{25}	32M	35	2^{35}	32G	45	2^{45}	32T
26	2^{26}	64M	36	2^{36}	64G	46	2^{46}	64T
27	2^{27}	128M	37	2^{37}	128G	47	2^{47}	128T
28	2^{28}	256M	38	2^{38}	256G	48	2^{48}	256T
29	2^{29}	512M	39	2^{39}	512G	49	2^{49}	512T

Table 1.3: Nonnegative powers of 2 up to 512T

Again, in reality, the analogy is not exact. For example, 2^{20} = 1048576 which clearly is not precisely 10^6. On the other hand, when the approximation is applied, the sequence 1, 2, 4, 8, 16, 32, 64, 128, 256, 512 naturally repeats for any of the multipliers K, M, G, T and so on.

In summary, in order to truly develop expertise with binary numbers, it is ***imperative*** that one memorize and have a basic, intuitive understanding of powers of two.

Chapter Two: Review of Unsigned Base 10 Integers

Let us first address some language that will be applied through this development:

The word 'unsigned' means 'nonnegative'.

In other words, the term 'unsigned' refers to numbers that are either zero or positive. Nonnegative is a mathematical term, and, 'unsigned' is more of a computer science term oftentimes reserved to describe specific variable types. By extension, the word '**signed**' is then used to encompass both nonnegative and negative numbers. We will begin our discussion by considering only unsigned integers. Only after these concepts are mastered will we move on to consider signed integers.

In order to understand binary numbers (i.e. numbers in base 2), it will be helpful to review our understanding of base 10 numbers. Since we will be appealing to knowledge that was most likely instilled somewhere during early elementary school, this review will appear deceptively simple. However, please pay close attention, all the principles for expanding a number in any base are rooted in the formulation provided in this section.

Important note: For better or for worse, the word '**decimal**' is sometimes used to refer to numbers in base 10.

When one expresses a number in base 10, it is assumed that a number will be expressed using digits from the allowed set of 10 symbols:

$$\{0,1,2,3,4,5,6,7,8,9\}$$

Since the application we have in mind is for computer systems, we must be mindful of the fact that _computer systems are necessarily limited to a finite number of digits_. Therefore, we will examine unsigned base 10 integers for various numbers of digits in order to illustrate a repeatable pattern that can easily be extended to other bases (such as base 2). We will be using the letter 'm' to indicate the number of digits.

One digit (m=1):

x 10^0		
x 1		**Result**
0	= 0 x 10^0	= 0
1	= 1 x 10^0	= 1
2	= 2 x 10^0	= 2
.	.	.
.	.	.
.	.	.
8	= 8 x 10^0	= 8
9	= 9 x 10^0	= 9

Table 2.1: The set of all one digit nonnegative decimal integers

In this case the multiplier for the single digit is assumed to be 10^0 (which refers to the so-called 'ones' place). Observe, that with m=1 digit in base 10, it is possible to represent 10^1 numbers counting from 0 to $10^1-1=9$.

Two digits (m=2):

x 10^1	x 10^0		
x 10	x 1		Result
0	0	= 0 x 10^1 + 0 x 10^0	= 0
0	1	= 0 x 10^1 + 1 x 10^0	= 1
0	2	= 0 x 10^1 + 2 x 10^0	= 2
.	.	.	.
.	.	.	.
.	.	.	.
0	8	= 0 x 10^1 + 8 x 10^0	= 8
0	9	= 0 x 10^1 + 9 x 10^0	= 9
1	0	= 1 x 10^1 + 0 x 10^0	= 10
1	1	= 1 x 10^1 + 1 x 10^0	= 11
.	.	.	.
.	.	.	.
.	.	.	.
9	8	= 9 x 10^1 + 8 x 10^0	= 98
9	9	= 9 x 10^1 + 9 x 10^0	= 99

Table 2.2: The set of all two digit unsigned decimal integers

In this case, the multipliers are assumed to be 10^0 and 10^1 (which refer to the 'ones' place and the 'tens' place). Observe, that with m=2 digits in base 10, it is possible to represent 10^2 numbers counting from 0 to $10^2-1=99$.

Three digits (m=3):

x 10^2	x 10^1	x 10^0		
x 100	x 10	x 1		Result
0	0	0	= 0 x 10^2 + 0 x 10^1 + 0 x 10^0	= 0
0	0	1	= 0 x 10^2 + 0 x 10^1 + 1 x 10^0	= 1
0	0	2	= 0 x 10^2 + 0 x 10^1 + 2 x 10^0	= 2
.	.	.	.	.
.	.	.		.
.	.	.	.	.
3	0	8	= 3 x 10^2 + 0 x 10^1 + 8 x 10^0	= 308
3	0	9	= 3 x 10^2 + 0 x 10^1 + 9 x 10^0	= 309
3	1	0	= 3 x 10^2 + 1 x 10^1 + 0 x 10^0	= 310
3	1	1	= 3 x 10^2 + 1 x 10^1 + 1 x 10^0	= 311
.	.	.	.	.
.	.	.		.
.	.	.	.	.
9	9	8	= 9 x 10^2 + 9 x 10^1 + 8 x 10^0	= 998
9	9	9	= 9 x 10^2 + 9 x 10^1 + 9 x 10^0	= 999

Table 2.3: The set of all three digit unsigned decimal integers

In this case, the multipliers are assumed to be 10^0, 10^1 and 10^2 (which refer to the 'ones' place, the 'tens' place and the 'hundreds' place).

Observe, that with m=3 digits in base 10, it is possible to represent 10^3 numbers counting from 0 to 10^3-1=999.

We invoke these expansions so readily and so naturally that we do not even think about it anymore. For example, while it is true that
$$(1021)_{10} = 1 \times 10^3 + 0 \times 10^2 + 2 \times 10^1 + 1 \times 10^0,$$
most would prefer to see their banking statements presented using the _shorthand form on the left side_ of the '=' sign. _For the purposes of computer systems and binary numbers_, we will be equally concerned with the expansion on the right side of the '=' sign.

We must, therefore, highlight and summarize some important takeaways from the above tables that will be extrapolated to other base expansions:

1. Base 10 numbers are expressed using the allowed set of 10 symbols:
   {0,1,2,3,4,5,6,7,8,9}
2. Using powers of 10, each position in the number is assigned a specific '**weight**' (e.g. the ones place, the tens place and so on).
3. Assuming an unsigned integer with 'm' digits, the leftmost digit has the greatest weight equal to 10^{m-1} and rightmost digit has the least weight equal to 10^0.
   a. The leftmost digit is sometimes referred to as the '**most significant digit**'.
   b. The rightmost digit is sometimes referred to as the '**least significant digit**'.
4. Assuming 'm' digits, it is possible to represent 10^m unsigned integers counting from 0 to $10^m - 1$.

From a combinatorial perspective, the 10^m result should be clear given that we have 10 symbols to choose from in each digit position. So, for example, with m=3 digits, this means that there are exactly (10)(10)(10)=10^3 possible **unique** decimal sequences that could be generated from the allowed symbol set {0,1,2,3,4,5,6,7,8,9}. It is extremely critical to note that this combinatorial result is independent of how we arrange those base 10 sequences. For the time being, we are discussing **unsigned integers** meaning that we have chosen to arrange the complete set of 10^m unique sequences by counting from zero to 10^m-1.

Extension to other bases

As an interesting exercise, let us extend the above conclusions regarding unsigned integers to base 3. In this case, the allowed set of 3 symbols will, by convention, taken to be: **{0,1,2}**. Using 'm' positions, it is possible to represent 3^m unsigned integers counting from 0 to 3^m-1.

Under these circumstance, invoking m=4 implies that we can count from 0 to $3^4-1=80$. For example,

$$(1021)_3 = 1 \times 3^3 + 0 \times 3^2 + 2 \times 3^1 + 1 \times 3^0$$
$$= 1 \times 27 + 0 \times 9 + 2 \times 3 + 1 \times 1$$
$$= 27 + 0 + 6 + 1$$
$$= (34)_{10}$$

where the conversion to base 10 occurs because we have expressed the powers of three as base 10 numbers.

Observe, if there are 34 chairs in a room, there always 34 chairs regardless if that number is expressed in base 10 as $(34)_{10}$ or in some other base such as base 3 written as $(1021)_3$. The main point is that when it comes to counting, the base expansion is simply a tool used to represent a specific numerical condition. It is often preferable to operate in base 10 because we are so used to simplifying arithmetic properties when using powers of 10; however, computer system applications are often more easily described using base 2.

Chapter Three: Unsigned Binary Integers

We are specifically interested in representing numbers in base 2 (so-called '**binary**' expansions). When one expresses a number in base 2, it is assumed to be expanded in powers of two using binary digits from the allowed set of 2 symbols:

$$\{0,1\}$$

We introduce some language that is used throughout the computer systems community:
The word 'bit' is a contraction of the term 'binary digit'.

In a manner similar to the decimal case previously described, we will examine unsigned binary integers for various numbers of bits in order to highlight a repeatable pattern that can be used to generate tables with any number of bits.

<u>One bit (m=1)</u>:

x 2^0		
x 1		(Result)$_{10}$
0	= 0 x 2^0	= 0
1	= 1 x 2^0	= 1

Table 3.1: The set of all one bit unsigned binary integers

In this case the multiplier for the single bit is assumed to be 2^0. Observe that, in base 2 with m=1 bit, it is possible to represent $2^1=2$ unsigned integers counting from 0 to $2^1-1=1$.

Two bits (m=2):

x 2^1	x 2^0		(Result)$_{10}$
x 2	x 1		
0	0	$= 0 \times 2^1 + 0 \times 2^0$	= 0
0	1	$= 0 \times 2^1 + 1 \times 2^0$	= 1
1	0	$= 1 \times 2^1 + 0 \times 2^0$	= 2
1	1	$= 1 \times 2^1 + 1 \times 2^0$	= 3

Table 3.2: The set of all two bit unsigned binary integers

In this case, the multipliers are assumed to be 2^0 and 2^1. Observe that, in base 2 with m=2 bits, it is possible to represent $2^2=4$ unsigned integers counting from 0 to $2^2-1=3$. In addition, by convention, the leftmost bit has the greatest weight equal to 2^1 and rightmost bit has the least weight equal to 2^0.

<u>Three bits (m=3):</u>

x 2^2	x 2^1	x 2^0		
x 4	x 2	x 1		(Result)$_{10}$
0	0	0	$= 0 \times 2^2 + 0 \times 2^1 + 0 \times 2^0$	= 0
0	0	1	$= 0 \times 2^2 + 0 \times 2^1 + 1 \times 2^0$	= 1
0	1	0	$= 0 \times 2^2 + 1 \times 2^1 + 0 \times 2^0$	= 2
0	1	1	$= 0 \times 2^2 + 1 \times 2^1 + 1 \times 2^0$	= 3
1	0	0	$= 1 \times 2^2 + 0 \times 2^1 + 0 \times 2^0$	= 4
1	0	1	$= 1 \times 2^2 + 0 \times 2^1 + 1 \times 2^0$	= 5
1	1	0	$= 1 \times 2^2 + 1 \times 2^1 + 0 \times 2^0$	= 6
1	1	1	$= 1 \times 2^2 + 1 \times 2^1 + 1 \times 2^0$	= 7

Table 3.3: The set of all three bit unsigned binary integers

In this case, the multipliers are assumed to be 2^0, 2^1 and 2^2 (which refer to the 'ones' place, the 'twos' place and the 'fours' place). Observe that, with m=3 bits, it is possible to represent $2^3=8$ unsigned integers counting from 0 to $2^3-1=7$. In addition, by convention, the leftmost bit has the greatest weight equal to 2^2 and rightmost bit has the least weight equal to 2^0.

As with the decimal case, we have arrived at the following conclusions:

1. Binary numbers are expressed using the allowed set of 2 symbols: **{0,1}**
2. Using powers of 2, each position in the number is assigned a specific '**weight**' (e.g. the ones place, the 'twos' place, the 'fours' place, the 'eights' place and so on).
3. Assuming an unsigned integer with 'm' digits, the leftmost bit has the greatest weight equal to 2^{m-1} and rightmost bit has the least weight equal to 2^0.
   a. The leftmost bit is referred to as the '<u>**most significant bit**</u>' **(MSB)**.
   b. The rightmost bit is referred to as the '<u>**least significant bit**</u>' **(LSB).**
4. Assuming 'm' bits, one can represent 2^m unsigned integers counting from 0 to 2^m-1.

Again, from a combinatorial perspective, the 2^m result should be clear given that we have 2 symbols to choose from in each bit position. For example, with m=3 digits, this means that there are exactly $(2)(2)(2)=2^3=8$ possible **<u>unique</u>** binary sequences that can be generated from the allowed symbol set {0,1}. This combinatorial result is totally independent of how we *arrange* those base 2 sequences. For the time being, we are discussing **<u>unsigned integers</u>** meaning that we have *chosen to arrange the set of 2^m unique sequences* by counting from zero to 2^m-1.

Binary to Decimal Conversion

Conversion from base 2 to base 10 is quite straightforward as we demonstrate in the following examples.

Applying the above table, for m=3 bits,

$$(101)_2 = 1 \times 2^2 + 0 \times 2^1 + 1 \times 2^0$$
$$= 1 \times 4 + 0 \times 2 + 1 \times 1$$
$$= 4 + 0 + 1$$
$$= (5)_{10}$$

Observe that the *conversion from binary to base 10 naturally occurs* because we have chosen to express the powers of two as base 10 numbers.

As we increase the number of bits in our binary numbers, it should be clear that it will become impractical to list every possible binary number and read the desired value off the table. Therefore, being able to convert numbers from binary to decimal *requires being highly fluent with powers of two*.

Assuming m=4 bits,

$$(1011)_2 = 1 \times 2^3 + 0 \times 2^2 + 1 \times 2^1 + 1 \times 2^0$$
$$= 8 + 0 + 2 + 1$$
$$= (11)_{10}$$

Assuming m=12 bits,

$(100101111001)_2$

$= 1 \times 2^{11} + 0 \times 2^{10} + 0 \times 2^9 + 1 \times 2^8 + 0 \times 2^7$
$+ 1 \times 2^6 + 1 \times 2^5 + 1 \times 2^4 + 1 \times 2^3$
$+ 0 \times 2^2 + 0 \times 2^1 + 1 \times 2^0$

$= 1 \times 2048 + 0 \times 1024 + 0 \times 512 + 1 \times 256 + 0 \times 128$
$+ 1 \times 64 + 1 \times 32 + 1 \times 16 + 1 \times 8$
$+ 0 \times 4 + 0 \times 2 + 1 \times 1$

$= 2048 + 256 + 64 + 32 + 16 + 8 + 1$

$= (2425)_{10}$

As one exercises enough examples, one should get used to using powers of two just as easily as being used to powers of ten with decimal numbers. Conversion from binary numbers to decimal numbers _requires being fluent at summing powers of two_ and can easily be visualized as the following examples demonstrate.

Assuming m=8 bits, consider converting $(10111010)_2$ to base 10:

2^7	2^6	2^5	2^4	2^3	2^2	2^1	2^0
128	64	32	16	8	4	2	1
1	0	1	1	1	0	1	0

Notice that we only need to consider the columns where the bit value is one (the zero values to do not contribute to the sum); hence,

$$(10111010)_2 = 128 + 32 + 16 + 8 + 2$$
$$= (186)_{10}$$

Assuming m=10 bits, consider converting $(1000000011)_2$ to base 10:

2^9	2^8	2^7	2^6	2^5	2^4	2^3	2^2	2^1	2^0
512	256	128	64	32	16	8	4	2	1
1	0	0	0	0	0	0	0	1	1

$$(1000000011)_2 = 512 + 2 + 1$$
$$= (515)_{10}$$

Given these examples, it should now be clear why fluency with powers of two is so important for understanding binary numbers.

Exercises:

Convert the following unsigned binary integers to their decimal values:

a. $(10000)_2 = (?)_{10}$

b. $(000100)_2 = (?)_{10}$

c. $(100001)_2 = (?)_{10}$

d. $(10101010)_2 = (?)_{10}$

e. $(1001011001)_2 = (?)_{10}$

f. $(00001011)_2 = (?)_{10}$

g. $(00010110)_2 = (?)_{10}$

h. $(00101100)_2 = (?)_{10}$

i. $(01011000)_2 = (?)_{10}$

Chapter Four: Important Observations I

The Table Pattern

It is a simple matter to generate lists of binary numbers similar to the ones shown in Tables 3.1-3.3 when considering the unsigned case. Let us revisit the m=3 table

Binary	Decimal
000	0
001	1
010	2
011	3
100	4
101	5
110	6
111	7

Starting with the most significant bit, observe that the leftmost column in the binary expansion has half the list of binary sequences starting with zero and half the list starting with one. Then, as we move from left to right, a pattern develops as the next column always halves the number of zeros and ones.

Based upon this observation, it should be possible to generate an m-bit table of all possible unique binary sequences very quickly simply by listing the columns and adhering to the pattern.

Let us try this for the case where m=4:

Binary	Decimal		Binary	Decimal
0000	0		1000	8
0001	1		1001	9
0010	2		1010	10
0011	3		1011	11
0100	4		1100	12
0101	5		1101	13
0110	6		1110	14
0111	7		1111	15

This table is generated column by column starting with 8 zeros and 8 ones in the most significant bit. The next column applies 4 zeros and 4 ones. The next column applies 2 zeros and 2 ones and so on. Notice that this 4 bit table naturally counts in decimal from 0 to $2^4-1=15$.

As a side note, the self-similarity of the counting process dictates that the m=3 bit table be contained within the m=4 table, and the m=2 bit table be naturally contained within the m=3 table and so on. This fact can be used as a check to make sure that you have correctly generated a table for the desired number of bits.

Exercise:

In a manner similar to the m=4 case shown above, generate a table of unsigned integers for the m=5 case using the column by column pattern. Check various entries in your table to ensure that the binary values correspond to the correct decimal values.

Maximum/Minimum Values

It is extremely important to get used to recognizing certain binary sequences containing 'm' bits. For the unsigned case, the minimum value in decimal is always $(0)_{10}$ and the maximum value must be $(2^m-1)_{10}$. When expressed in base 2, the minimum value will be a string of 'm' zeros and the maximum value will be a string of 'm' ones. Consider the following table where each row shows the minimum and maximum unsigned values assuming different numbers of bits in the representation:

m	Minimum Value in base 10	Minimum Value in base 2	Maximum Value in base 10	Maximum Value in base 2
4	0	0000	$2^4-1=15$	1111
8	0	0000 0000	$2^8-1=255$	1111 1111
11	0	000 0000 0000	$2^{11}-1=2047$	111 1111 1111

Therefore, it should be a very, very, very straightforward exercise to determine the minimum and maximum unsigned values when the number of bits 'm' is specified. At first glance, asking what is the maximum unsigned value that can be represented using m=20 bits could seem like a daunting task. However, the present discussion makes the answer attainable in less than five seconds:

$$(2^{20}-1)_{10} = (1111\ 1111\ 1111\ 1111\ 1111)_2$$

Oddness/Evenness

Now that we have a catalog of unsigned binary integers for the m=1 bit through the m=5 bit case. A cursory inspection of these catalog immediately shows us how to distinguish between odd numbers and even numbers by considering only the least significant bit (i.e. the 'ones' place).

Observation:
- The least significant bit (LSB) for even numbers is always zero.
- The least significant bit (LSB) for odd numbers is always one.

To see why this is so, let's momentarily leave the LSB out of the conversation. Since we know that the sum of a set of even numbers always results in an even number, it should be clear that summing any combination of positive powers of two must result in an even number. Now, if the LSB is equal to zero, then the sum will remain even; however, if the LSB is equal to one, then the sum will become odd because a one has been added to an even number.

Notice that the binary number system is a much more natural numerical reference frame to define the binary condition of evenness versus oddness. For example, with decimal numbers one must detect a least significant digit within the set {0,2,4,6,8} for evenness or a least significant digit within the set {1,3,5,7,9} for oddness. Both bases provide demonstrably equivalent descriptions; however, computer operations often involve inspecting bit values in specific positions. A single measurement of the LSB is clearly more efficient than checking a multitude of cases to detect oddness versus evenness.

There is an even deeper, more pressing reason for understanding oddness/evenness via the LSB of a binary expansion. It has to do with computing the remainder after dividing an integer by 2 (i.e. the **remainder modulo 2** or just **mod 2** for the sake of brevity). When we divide a number by two, the only two possible answers for the remainder are either zero or one:

$$3 \bmod 2 = 1$$
$$4 \bmod 2 = 0$$
$$5 \bmod 2 = 1$$
$$6 \bmod 2 = 0$$
$$7 \bmod 2 = 1$$

Observation:
- Taking any number mod 2 is equivalent to determining oddness/evenness
- Given an unsigned integer 'N':
  N mod 2 = LSB of the binary expansion of N

Multiplication and Division by 2

Recall what happens in base 10 whenever we multiply or divide a number by 10. Assuming m=4 digits:

$$10 \times 0003 = 0030$$
$$10 \times 0030 = 0300$$
$$10 \times 0300 = 3000$$

Notice that multiplication by 10 results in shifting the decimal sequence to the left by one digit and division by will shift the decimal sequence to the right.

This result is true for any base expansion, but we are particularly interested in the binary case. So let's verify this result for an m=5 example base 2:

$$2 \times (00001)_2 = (00010)_2 = (2)_{10}$$
$$2 \times (00010)_2 = (00100)_2 = (4)_{10}$$
$$2 \times (00100)_2 = (01000)_2 = (8)_{10}$$
$$2 \times (01000)_2 = (10000)_2 = (16)_{10}$$

Observation:

- *Multiplying a number by 2* in base 2 is equivalent to a *left shift* of the binary sequence by one bit
- *Dividing a number by 2* in base 2 is equivalent to a *right shift* of the binary sequence by one bit

Remember that integer division must always result in an integer (and a remainder). Hence, when calculating 3/2 (which results in the fractional number 1.5), integer division implies that we must drop the fractional part after the right shift.

Therefore, for m=4 bits,

$\qquad (1100)_2 / 2 = (0110)_2 = (6)_{10}$ (right shift)

$\qquad (0110)_2 / 2 = (0011)_2 = (3)_{10}$ (right shift)

$\qquad (0011)_2 / 2 = (0001)_2 = (1)_{10}$ (right shift with fractional part dropped)

For the purposes of this introductory text, we are focused on understanding binary integers. Fractional numbers invite a deeper discussion and will therefore be presented in a subsequent volume.

The key take away from the above observation is to understand the relationship between multiplication by 2 and left shifts of binary sequences (as well as division by 2 and right shifts of binary sequences). Now go back and revisit the exercises already presented for performing binary to decimal conversion. You should be able to see that some of them were designed to demonstrate these principles.

Exercises:
1. Identify the largest unsigned integer that can be represented on a computer that processes
   a. 32-bit unsigned integers
   b. 64-bit unsigned integers

   Express your answers in both base 2 and base 10. Are these values odd or even?

2. Explain why, when the bit pattern '101' is encountered in an unsigned binary integer, the decimal value of this pattern should be a multiple of $(10)_{10}$ (Hint: start with $(0000000101)_2$ and perform successive left shifts).

Chapter Five: Decimal to Binary Conversion

We have already seen how perform binary to decimal conversion by summing powers of two in the appropriate bit locations. Now we can discuss the inverse process of converting decimal values to binary numbers. We introduce three different approaches, each with increasing levels of sophistication:

- ad hoc intuition
- basic algorithm
- base expansion algorithm

Ad hoc intuition

The game is to try and find the correct combination of powers of two that will sum to the decimal value. To do this, we must make sure that an appropriate number of bits has been specified. For example, let's try to convert $(24)_{10}$ to its binary value. We know that $0 \leq 24 \leq 2^5-1$; hence, we require at least 5 bits to represent the number. Let's assume m=7 bits and try to find the powers of two that will sum to 24.

$$24 = 16 + 8 = (001\ 1000)_2$$

Let's try some more assuming m=7 bits

$$65 = 64 + 1 = (100\ 0001)_2$$
$$35 = 32 + 2 + 1 = (010\ 0011)_2$$
$$57 = 32 + 16 + 8 + 1 = (011\ 1001)_2$$

Moving up to higher numbers of bits will require fluency with summing powers of two. For example, assuming m=16 bits

$$2049 = 2048 + 1 = (0000\ 1000\ 0000\ 0001)_2$$
$$32770 = 32768 + 2 = (1000\ 0000\ 0000\ 0010)_2$$
$$8216 = 8192 + 16 + 8 = (0010\ 0000\ 0001\ 1000)_2$$

and so on.

Basic Algorithm

It is important to have intuition regarding binary expansions as discussed above. However, such an approach can become tedious for large numbers of bits unless some repeatable method can be applied that will work for any binary sequence. Here is a suggestion given some unsigned integer 'n' where $0 \leq n \leq 2^m-1$ and 'm' is assumed to be greater than or equal to 1.

1. Set: b=[ ] (i.e. 'b' is an empty binary string)
2. Set: k=m-1
3. If $n < 2^k$

   b=[b, 0] (i.e. concatenate a zero to the binary string 'b')

   Else

   b=[b, 1] (i.e. concatenate a one to the binary string 'b')
4. Set: $p = n - 2^k$
5. If $p \geq 0$

   Set: n=p
6. Set: k=k-1
7. if $k \geq 0$, then go to step 3
8. stop

This is a simple iterative algorithm that works by peeling off successively powers of two in decreasing order and can be easily programmed with a construct such as a 'for' or 'while' loop. Let's look at an example and walk through each iteration when n=9 and m=4 bits are the assumed values (clearly, $0 \leq 9 \leq 2^4-1$):

Iteration k=m-1=3:
  a. $9 \geq 2^3$ ➜ b=[b, 1] = 1
  b. Set: $p = n - 2^k = 9 - 2^3 = 1$
  c. $p \geq 0$ ➜ set: n=1
  d. Set: k = k-1 = 2

Iteration k=2:
  a. $1 < 2^2$ ➜ b=[b, 0] = 10
  b. Set: $p = n - 2^k = 1 - 2^2 = -3$
  c. $p < 0$ ➜ n is left unchanged
  d. Set: k = k-1 = 1

Iteration k=1:
  a. $1 < 2^1$ ➜ b=[b, 0] = 100
  b. Set: $p = n - 2^k = 1 - 2^1 = -1$
  c. $p < 0$ ➜ n is left unchanged
  d. Set: k = k-1 = 0

Iteration k=0:
  a. $1 \geq 2^0$ ➜ b=[b, 1] = 1001
  b. Set: $p = n - 2^k = 1 - 2^0 = 0$
  c. $p \geq 0$ ➜ set: n=0
  d. Set: k = k-1 = -1
'stop' since k<0.
Hence, the above algorithm gives us the desired result that $(9)_{10} = (1001)_2$.

Exercise:
    Test other values of 'n' and 'm' to understand and internalize how this algorithm is working.

Base Expansion Algorithm

This is a slightly deeper algorithm even though the steps to this approach are quite straightforward. Given some unsigned integer 'n' where $0 \leq n \leq 2^m-1$ and 'm' is assumed to be greater than or equal to 1:

1. Set: K=2
2. Output: n mod 2
3. Set: n = integer part of n/K (i.e. integer division with integer result)
4. Set: m=m-1
5. If m > 0, then go to step 2
6. stop

Let's look at an example by walking through each iteration when n=11 and m=4 bits (clearly, $0 \leq 11 \leq 2^4-1$):

Iteration m=4:
   a. Output: 11 mod 2 = 1
   b. Set: n = integer part of 11/2 = 5
   c. Set: m = 4 - 1 = 3

Iteration m=3:
   a. Output: 5 mod 2 = 1
   b. Set: n = integer part of 5/2 = 2
   c. Set: m = 3 - 1 = 2

Iteration m=2:
   a. Output: 2 mod 2 = 0
   b. Set: n = integer part of 2/2 = 1
   c. Set: m = 2 - 1 = 1

Iteration m=1:
  a. Output: 1 mod 2 = 1
  b. Set: n = integer part of 1/2 = 0
  c. Set: m = 1 - 1 = 0
'stop' since m≤0.

Notice that *this algorithm outputs bit values from LSB first to MSB last*: 1101. Hence, we end up with the desired result that $(11)_{10} = (1011)_2$.

Exercise:
  Test other values of 'n' and 'm' to internalize how this algorithm is working.

Although the steps are easily implemented, in order to *fully appreciate why this algorithm works*, it is necessary to reference the sections previously introduced dealing with oddness/evenness and divide/right shift concepts. Specifically, step 2 computes 'n mod 2' which we know is a calculation that inspects the LSB to determine if it is a zero or a one (i.e. odd or even). In addition, division by two in step 3 is equivalent to a right shift of the binary representation. Taken together this algorithm is easily phrased as follows:
  1. Output the LSB
  2. Right shift the number
  3. Go to step 1 until all 'm' bits are output.

It is important to point out that the above algorithm works for any base value K. For our purposes we have set K=2 for the case of binary numbers. However, computing n modulo K in step 2 must always result in a remainder from the allowed symbol set {0,1,2, ..., K-1}; and, division by K in step 3 is always a right shift by one digit in base K.

Exercise:

For K=3, $n = (31)_{10} = (1021)_3$. Prove to yourself that the above algorithm works in base 3 by converting the decimal value to the base 3 ('ternary') value assuming the allowed symbol set {0,1,2} with m=4 digits.

Chapter Six: Unsigned Binary Addition

Binary addition works exactly the same way as the decimal case except that the allowed set of symbols comes from the set {0,1}. Initially, this point can take a bit of getting used to in the event that a carry is generated in response to computing a sum. The following table shows the sum of two bits 'a' and 'b' for the four possible cases:

a	b		Carry Out	Sum
0	0		0	0
0	1		0	1
1	0		0	1
1	1		1	0

The first three rows generate the sums 0+0=0, 0+1=1 and 1+0=1. For the last case, we know that 1+1=2 in decimal and 1+1=10 in binary; hence, this sum requires _two_ bits to describe the result. In a manner similar to the decimal case, the _sum must carry over_ (i.e. 'carry out') to the next bit position in order to reflect the correct result. Therefore, the binary case is best phrased with at least m=2 positions:

Binary   Decimal

Carry 1
     01   1
+ 01   + 1
   10   2

This calculation reflects the information in the above table showing that when 'a' and 'b' are both equal to one, a 'carry out' value of one will be generated from the sum; otherwise, the carry out will be equal to zero. Notice that for binary numbers the values for the carry out can only come from the allowed set $\{0,1\}$.

Consider another example using m=4 bits and make sure you see how the carry works in base 2.

	Binary	Decimal
Carry	1 0 0	1
	0110	06
	+ 0101	+ 05
	1011	11

The key point to notice is that when summing the bits in a specific column, the carry out from the previous column position must be taken into account.

This implies that we should be prepared to compute the *sum of three bits* in each column. In order to enumerate all possible cases for the sum of three bits, we choose to introduce some terminology in order to keep track of the carry values. Assuming we are computing the sum within a specific column:

- **Carry In** = carry value from the *previous* column
- **Carry Out** = value to be carried to the *next* column

Note: Observe that the 'carry in' to the **LSB** is always assumed to be zero. For the purposes of this current discussion, we will omit explicitly writing the zero as a carry in to the LSB. Please bear in mind that this point would be highly relevant if one were to consider designing a digital system to perform binary addition.

Using the above terminology we can enumerate the sum of three bits for all possible $2^3=8$ cases:

Carry In	a	b	Carry Out	Sum
0	0	0	0	0
0	0	1	0	1
0	1	0	0	1
0	1	1	1	0
1	0	0	0	1
1	0	1	1	0
1	1	0	1	0
1	1	1	1	1

By taking the carry out into account, observe that 1+1 stills equals two and $1+1+1=(3)_{10} = (11)_2$.

Let's apply this information to an example:

Binary	Decimal
Carry 0 1 1	1
1011	11
+ 0011	+ 03
1110	14

As long as the value for the carry is properly accounted for, binary addition is simply a special case of what you already know how to do with decimal numbers.

Try some for yourself:

Binary	Decimal
Carry	1
0111	07
+ 0100	+ 04
	11

Binary	Decimal
Carry	1
0101	05
+ 0111	+ 07
	12

Notice how the decimal value can be used to double check the binary arithmetic. This is usually a good idea until one becomes fluent with binary addition.

The Carry Condition

For the purposes of computer system applications, the number of bits 'm' reserved for number representations is always finite and limited by the *precision* of the system design (e.g. 64 bits, 128 bits, 256 bits, etc). This is why it is so important to know the maximum value and minimum values that can be represented. As discussed previously, given 'm' bits, we know that the maximum unsigned integer is $(2^m-1)_{10}$. If the sum of two unsigned integers exceeds this value, it is important to 'flag' the fact that another bit of precision is required to handle the sum.

Consider an example for a computer with m=4 bits of integer precision. We know that the maximum value that can be represented is $(2^4-1)_{10} = (15)_{10} = (1111)_2$.

```
Carry 0 0 0              1
       1001             09
     + 1000           + 08
      10001             17
```

In this example, four bits are not enough to handle the addition.

With the finite integer precision, we choose to **introduce a 'carry' flag (C) for binary addition** to indicate when more bits are needed for the unsigned addition:

- If enough bits are available to add two unsigned numbers: set C=0
- If not enough bits available to add two unsigned numbers: set C=1

More directly:

- **C=1** if the sum of **all** the bits in the MSB column generates a carry out
- **C=0** Otherwise

Let's also introduce some more language that is used throughout the computer systems community:
The word '<u>byte</u>' refers to a set of 8-bits.

Let's consider a few more examples and increase the number of bits to m=8 (i.e. **1 byte**) so we start to get used to larger binary numbers (be aware that the maximum value is $(2^8-1)_{10} = (255)_{10} = (1111\ 1111)_2$).

```
Carry 0 0 0 0 0 0 0              0 1
      0111 1111                  127
    + 1000 0000                + 128
C=0   1111 1111                  255
```

```
Carry 0 0 0 0 0 0 0              0 1
      1000 0000                  128
    + 1000 0000                + 128
C=1   0000 0000                  256
```

```
Carry                           1 0
      1010 0000                  160
    + 0011 0000                + 048
C=                               208
```

```
Carry                           0 1
      1111 1110                  254
    + 0001 0011                + 019
C=                               273
```

Unsigned Multiplication

Consider multiplying two unsigned integers in base 10:

```
      312
    x 201
      312
      000
      624___
    62712
```

The same '*shift and add*' approach can be applied to unsigned binary integers:

```
      011
    x 101
      011
      000
      011__
    01111
```

(in decimal, 5 x 3 = 15)

Exercises

1. For m=8, perform the unsigned binary addition of $(125)_{10} + (25)_{10}$. Make sure you indicate the value of the C flag.

2. For m=8, perform the unsigned binary addition of $(108)_{10} + (58)_{10}$. Make sure you indicate the value of the C flag.

3. Construct your own example of multiplying two unsigned integers. What is the minimum number of bits required to store the product of two unsigned m-bit numbers?

4. Given m=21 bits
   a. Express $a=(2^{20}-1)_{10}$ as an unsigned binary integer
   b. Express $b=(1)_{10}$ as an unsigned binary integer
   c. Performed the unsigned binary addition: a+b. Make sure your answer is consistent with what you would expect by adding the base 10 values.

Chapter Seven: Hexadecimal Representation

Hexadecimal simply means base 16. The hexadecimal representation will prove convenient as a form of shorthand for long binary numbers with large numbers of bits. Working in base 16 implies that we must agree upon 16 allowed symbols which can be used to count from 0 to 15. By convention, virtually all computer systems agree on the following symbol set:

$$\{0,1,2,3,4,5,6,7,8,9,A,B,C,D,E,F\}$$

where

$$(A)_{16} = (10)_{10}, \quad (B)_{16} = (11)_{10}, \quad (C)_{16} = (12)_{10},$$
$$(D)_{16} = (13)_{10}, \quad (E)_{16} = (14)_{10}, \quad (F)_{16} = (15)_{10}$$

While not conceptually difficult, the letter to numerical translation can take some getting used to for those seeing this for the first time. In order to get used to this representation, let's try building some tables similar to our approach for base 10 and base 2.

One digit (m=1):

x 16^0		
x 1		(Result)$_{10}$
0	= 0 x 16^0	= 0
1	= 1 x 16^0	= 1
2	= 2 x 16^0	= 2
.	.	.
.	.	.
.	.	.
8	= 8 x 16^0	= 8
9	= 9 x 16^0	= 9
A	= 10 x 16^0	= 10
B	= 11 x 16^0	= 11
C	= 12 x 16^0	= 12
D	= 13 x 16^0	= 13
E	= 14 x 16^0	= 14
F	= 15 x 16^0	= 15

Table 7.1: The set of all one digit nonnegative hexadecimal integers

In this case the multiplier for the single digit is assumed to be 16^0. Observe that, in base 16 with m=1 digit, it is possible to represent 16^1=16 unsigned integers counting from 0 to 16^1-1=15.

Two digits (m=2):

x 16^1	x 16^0		
x 16	**x 1**		**(Result)$_{10}$**
0	0	= 0 x 16^1 + 0 x 16^0	= 0
0	1	= 0 x 16^1 + 1 x 16^0	= 1
0	2	= 0 x 16^1 + 2 x 16^0	= 2
.	.	.	.
.	.	.	.
0	8	= 0 x 16^1 + 8 x 16^0	= 8
0	9	= 0 x 16^1 + 9 x 16^0	= 9
0	A	= 0 x 16^1 + A x 16^0	= 10
.	.	.	.
.	.	.	.
0	E	= 0 x 16^1 + E x 16^0	= 14
0	F	= 0 x 16^1 + F x 16^0	= 15
1	0	= 1 x 16^1 + 0 x 16^0	= 16
1	1	= 1 x 16^1 + 1 x 16^0	= 17
1	2	= 1 x 16^1 + 2 x 16^0	= 18
.	.	.	.
.	.	.	.
F	C	= F x 16^1 + C x 16^0	= 252
F	D	= F x 16^1 + D x 16^0	= 253
F	E	= F x 16^1 + E x 16^0	= 254
F	F	= F x 16^1 + F x 16^0	= 255

Table 7.2: The set of all two digit nonnegative hexadecimal integers

In this case, the multipliers are assumed to be 16^0 and 16^1. Observe that, in base 16 with m=2 digits, it is possible to represent 16^2=256 unsigned integers which are ordered to count from 0 to 16^2-1=255. In addition, by convention, the leftmost bit has the greatest weight equal to 16^1 and rightmost bit has the least weight equal to 16^0.

<u>Three digits (m=3):</u>

x 16^2	x 16^1	x 16^0		(Result)$_{10}$
x 256	x 16	x 1		
0	0	0	= 0 x 16^2 + 0 x 16^1 + 0 x 16^0	= 0
0	0	1	= 0 x 16^2 + 0 x 16^1 + 1 x 16^0	= 1
0	0	2	= 0 x 16^2 + 0 x 16^1 + 2 x 16^0	= 2
.	.	.	.	.
A	0	E	= A x 16^2 + 0 x 16^1 + E x 16^0	= 2574
A	0	F	= A x 16^2 + 0 x 16^1 + F x 16^0	= 2575
A	1	0	= A x 16^2 + 1 x 16^1 + 0 x 16^0	= 2576
A	1	1	= A x 16^2 + 1 x 16^1 + 1 x 16^0	= 2577
.	.	.	.	.
F	F	E	= F x 16^2 + F x 16^1 + E x 16^0	= 4094
F	F	F	= F x 16^2 + F x 16^1 + F x 16^0	= 4095

Table 7.3: The set of all three digit nonnegative hexadecimal integers

In this case, the multipliers are assumed to be 16^0, 16^1 and 16^2 (which refer to the 'ones' place, the '16s' place and the '256s' place). Observe that, with m=3 bits, it is possible to represent $16^3=4096$ unsigned integers counting from 0 to $16^3-1=4095$. In addition, by convention, the leftmost bit has the greatest weight equal to 16^2 and rightmost bit has the least weight equal to 16^0.

We once again have arrived at several conclusions:

1. Hexadecimal numbers are expressed using the allowed set of 16 symbols:

   {0,1,2,3,4,5,6,7,8,9,A,B,C,D,E,F}

2. Using powers of 16, each position in the number is assigned a specific '**weight**' (e.g. the ones place, the '16s' place, the '256s' place, the '4096s' place and so on).

3. Assuming 'm' bits, one can represent 16^m nonnegative integers counting from 0 to 16^m-1.

4. Assuming an unsigned integer with 'm' hexadecimal digits, the leftmost digit has the greatest weight equal to 16^{m-1} and rightmost bit has the least weight equal to 16^0.

Once again, from a combinatorial perspective, the 16^m result should be clear given that we have 16 symbols to choose from in each bit position. For example, with m=3 digits, this means that there are exactly $(16)(16)(16)=16^3=4096$ possible **unique** hexadecimal sequences that could be generated from the allowed set of 16 symbols.

Hexadecimal to Decimal Conversion

Conversion from base 16 to base 10 is quite straightforward as we demonstrate in the following examples.

$$(10)_{16} = 1 \times 16^1 + 0 \times 16^0$$
$$= (16)_{10}$$

$$(11)_{16} = 1 \times 16^1 + 1 \times 16^0$$
$$= 16 + 1$$
$$= (17)_{10}$$

$$(22)_{16} = 2 \times 16^1 + 0 \times 16^0$$
$$= 32 + 2$$
$$= (34)_{10}$$

$$(A0F)_{16} = A \times 16^2 + 0 \times 16^1 + F \times 16^0$$
$$= 2560 + 15$$
$$= (2575)_{10}$$

$$(FFE)_{16} = F \times 16^2 + F \times 16^1 + E \times 16^0$$
$$= (4094)_{10}$$

Observe that the *conversion from base 16 to base 10 naturally occurs* because we have chosen to express the powers of 16 as base 10 numbers. Being able to convert numbers from hexadecimal to decimal *requires being fluent with powers of 16*.

Powers of 16

The rules for exponents allow us to apply our intuition regarding powers of two and apply it to powers of 16. The fact that $16=2^4$ allows us to quickly enumerate positive powers of 16 as shown in the following table.

n	$16^n = (2^4)^n = 2^{4n}$	=
0	$16^0 = (2^4)^0 = 2^0$	1
1	$16^1 = (2^4)^1 = 2^4$	16
2	$16^2 = (2^4)^2 = 2^8$	256
3	$16^3 = (2^4)^3 = 2^{12}$	4096
4	$16^4 = (2^4)^4 = 2^{16}$	65536
5	$16^5 = (2^4)^5 = 2^{20}$	1048576

.

Exercises

Convert the following hexadecimal numbers to base 10

a. $(AEEF)_{16} = (?)_{10}$

b. $(10111)_{16} = (?)_{10}$

c. $(CC9B21)_{16} = (?)_{10}$

Chapter Eight: Important Observations II

Maximum/Minimum Hexadecimal Values

Given 'm' digits the minimum nonnegative value is 0 and the maximum value is 16^m-1. From the above tables, we see the following

m	Minimum Value in base 10	Minimum Value in base 16	Maximum Value in base 10	Maximum Value in base 16
1	0	0	16^1-1=15	F
2	0	00	16^2-1=255	FF
3	0	000	16^3-1=4095	FFF

By extrapolation, the following should be clear when nonnegative integers are expressed in base 16,
- the minimum value will be a string of 'm' zeros
- the maximum value will be a string of 'm' Fs.

Counting in Hexadecimal

When counting with decimal numbers, we are used to reverting back to zero in any given column when we reach a decimal 9. For example, consider the counting sequence

...18, 19, 20, 21, ...

In order to count from 19 to 20 in base 10, the 9 reverts back zero and the next digit column is increased from one to two. This is a natural consequence of the fact that counting simply means adding one to a given value.

When counting with hexadecimal numbers, the key point to get used to is that we _revert back to zero when an 'F' is reached_ in any given column. For example, consider the counting sequence

...18, 19, 1A, 1B, 1C, 1D, 1E, 1F, 20, 21, ...

In order to count from 1F to 20, the F must revert back zero and the next digit column must be incremented from one to two.

Unsigned Hexadecimal Addition:

The principals for the carry extend quite naturally for the hexadecimal case. One simply needs to get used to the representation. Let's consider some examples.

Hexadecimal	Decimal
Carry 0	0 1
7F	127
+80	+128
FF	255

When first starting out, always remember to check that the hexadecimal result is consistent with the decimal addition.

Hexadecimal	Decimal
Carry 1	0 1
FE	254
+13	+019
1 11	273

(To see this, observe that $(E+3)_{16} = (17)_{10} = (11)_{16}$ and $(1+F+1)_{16} = (17)_{10} = (11)_{16})$

Hexadecimal	Decimal

Carry 0   0 1
    80   128
  +80   +128
  1 00   256

Carry 0   1 0
    A0   160
  +30   +048
                                208

Relationship Between Hexadecimal and Binary Numbers

A major reason for introducing the hexadecimal representation is that it can be used to shorten the length of a long binary sequence. Since the hexadecimal digits count from 0 to 15, this means that we can relate them to four bits binary numbers as follows

Hexadecimal	Binary	Decimal
0	0000	0
1	0001	1
2	0010	2
3	0011	3
4	0100	4
5	0101	5
6	0110	6
7	0111	7
8	1000	8
9	1001	9
A	1010	10
B	1011	11
C	1100	12
D	1101	13
E	1110	14
F	1111	15

.

Conversion from hexadecimal to binary and vice versa then becomes *an extremely simple process*:

- **Conversion from hexadecimal to binary**: for each hexadecimal digit, substitute the appropriate four bit binary sequence.
- **Conversion from binary to hexadecimal**: divide the binary number up into sets of fours bits, for each four bit binary sequence substitute the appropriate hexadecimal digit

Here are some examples that should make clear why hexadecimal is a useful shorthand representation for a binary number

$$(11100111)_2 = (1110\ 0111)_2 = (E7)_{16}$$
$$(0111101)_2 = (0011\ 1101)_2 = (3D)_{16}$$
$$(101101011100011)_2$$
$$= (0101\ 1010\ 1110\ 0011)_2$$
$$= (5AE3)_{16}$$

Notice that no reference to base 10 is being made. It is the relationship between powers of 2 and powers of 16 that allow us to seamlessly jump back and forth between binary and hexadecimal.

Hexadecimal	Binary	Decimal
Carry 0 1 1	0 1 0 0 0 1 1 1 1 1 1 1 1 1 0	
AOFE	1010 0000 1111 1110	41214
+ 2B23	+ 0010 1011 0010 0011	+ 11043
CC21	C=0 1100 1100 0010 0001	52257

Exercises:

1. $(2E)_{16} = (\ ? \ )_2$
2. $(F0)_{16} = (\ ? \ )_2$
3. $(A8)_{16} = (\ ? \ )_2$
4. $(A1E)_{16} = (\ ? \ )_2$
5. $(10010001)_2 = (\ ? \ )_{16} = (\ ? \ )_{10}$
6. $(111010)_2 = (\ ? \ )_{16} = (\ ? \ )_{10}$
7. $(1001000111110011)_2 = (\ ? \ )_{16} = (\ ? \ )_{10}$

8. What is the maximum unsigned value that can be represented using m=8 hexadecimal digits? What is this value in binary? What is this value in decimal?

9. Count from E1B0 to E1D0 in hexadecimal.

10. For m=8, perform **both** the hexadecimal and the unsigned binary addition of $(100)_{10} + (128)_{10}$. For the binary addition, make sure you indicate the value of the C flag.

Chapter Nine: Signed Two's Complement Binary Integers

Up to this point we have only considered unsigned (i.e. nonnegative) integers. With the unsigned representation, we have been able to introduce the addition of binary numbers. But what if we want to subtract? It is possible to define binary subtraction in a manner similar to decimal subtraction (just like we did for binary addition). In this case, we would have to keep track of the column-by-column difference as well as a possible 'borrow' from the relevant column. Rather than introduce such an approach, we can recognize that subtraction is merely the addition of negative numbers

$$a - b = a + (-b).$$

With this approach we can keep our binary addition methodology as fundamental (without any need for modification) and simply extend the set of binary numbers to include negative integers.

For this case, we review some language relevant to this development:

The word 'signed' refers to numbers that can take on both 'nonnegative' and 'negative' values .

While there are many possible choices for representing *signed integers*, we will focus on the so-called '**Signed Two's Complement Representation**' which is typically applied within most computer systems (for example, a variable of type 'int' declared in some given programming language adheres to the signed two's complement convention).

Given 'm' bits, we already know that there are exactly 2^m possible unique binary sequences that can be used to represent 2^m signed integers. A sensible strategy then is to take half of the list of 2^m possible sequences and use them to represent nonnegative numbers, and then use the other half to represent negative numbers.

Again, there are many ways to do this, but *in the <u>Signed 2's Complement Representation</u>:*
> *The desired distribution of numbers is achieved by multiplying the MSB in the unsigned binary expansion by -1.*

Once again, we will examine signed 2's complement integers for various numbers of bits in order to highlight a repeatable pattern that can be used to generate tables with any number of bits.

Two bits (m=2):

x (- 2^1)	x 2^0		(Result)$_{10}$
0	1	= 0 x (- 2^1) + 1 x 2^0	+1
0	0	= 0 x (- 2^1) + 0 x 2^0	0
1	1	= 1 x (- 2^1) + 1 x 2^0	-1
1	0	= 1 x (- 2^1) + 0 x 2^0	-2

Table 9.1: The set of all two bit signed 2's complement integers

Notice how **the weight of the MSB is multiplied by -1**. Also, pay close attention to how the set of $2^2=4$ unique binary sequences are distributed when compared with the unsigned case. Instead of counting from 0 to $2^2-1=3$, we are now able to count from $-2^1=-2$ to $2^1-1=+1$ where half of the available set of binary sequences (specifically, 00 and 01) are used for representing nonnegative integers and the other half (specifically, 10 and 11) are now used to represent negative integers.

Threes bit (m=3):

x (- 2^2)	x 2^1	x 2^0		(Result)$_{10}$
0	1	1	= 0 x (- 2^2) + 1 x 2^1 + 1 x 2^0	+3
0	1	0	= 0 x (- 2^2) + 1 x 2^1 + 0 x 2^0	+2
0	0	1	= 0 x (- 2^2) + 0 x 2^1 + 1 x 2^0	+1
0	0	0	= 0 x (- 2^2) + 0 x 2^1 + 0 x 2^0	0
1	1	1	= 1 x (- 2^2) + 1 x 2^1 + 1 x 2^0	-1
1	1	0	= 1 x (- 2^2) + 1 x 2^1 + 0 x 2^0	-2
1	0	1	= 1 x (- 2^2) + 0 x 2^1 + 1 x 2^0	-3
1	0	0	= 1 x (- 2^2) + 0 x 2^1 + 0 x 2^0	-4

Table 9.2: The set of all three bit signed 2's complement integers

Again, in order to create the set of negative numbers *in this representation, the MSB in the binary expansion is multiplied by -1*. The set of 2^3=8 unique binary sequences are used to count from -2^2=-4 to 2^2-1=+3. In a manner similar to the unsigned case, try and see the pattern developing in the list of binary sequences. Also, pay close attention to how we are characterizing the maximum and minimum values that can be represented.

Four bits (m=4):

x (-2^3)	x 2^2	x 2^1	x 2^0		(Result)$_{10}$
0	1	1	1	$= 0 \times (-2^3) + 1 \times 2^2 + 1 \times 2^1 + 1 \times 2^0$	+7
0	1	1	0	$= 0 \times (-2^3) + 1 \times 2^2 + 1 \times 2^1 + 0 \times 2^0$	+6
0	1	0	1	$= 0 \times (-2^3) + 1 \times 2^2 + 0 \times 2^1 + 1 \times 2^0$	+5
0	1	0	0	$= 0 \times (-2^3) + 1 \times 2^2 + 0 \times 2^1 + 0 \times 2^0$	+4
0	0	1	1	$= 0 \times (-2^3) + 0 \times 2^2 + 1 \times 2^1 + 1 \times 2^0$	+3
0	0	1	0	$= 0 \times (-2^3) + 0 \times 2^2 + 1 \times 2^1 + 0 \times 2^0$	+2
0	0	0	1	$= 0 \times (-2^3) + 0 \times 2^2 + 0 \times 2^1 + 1 \times 2^0$	+1
0	0	0	0	$= 0 \times (-2^3) + 0 \times 2^2 + 0 \times 2^1 + 0 \times 2^0$	0
1	1	1	1	$= 1 \times (-2^3) + 1 \times 2^2 + 1 \times 2^1 + 1 \times 2^0$	-1
1	1	1	0	$= 1 \times (-2^3) + 1 \times 2^2 + 1 \times 2^1 + 0 \times 2^0$	-2
1	1	0	1	$= 1 \times (-2^3) + 1 \times 2^2 + 0 \times 2^1 + 1 \times 2^0$	-3
1	1	0	0	$= 1 \times (-2^3) + 1 \times 2^2 + 0 \times 2^1 + 0 \times 2^0$	-4
1	0	1	1	$= 1 \times (-2^3) + 0 \times 2^2 + 1 \times 2^1 + 1 \times 2^0$	-5
1	0	1	0	$= 1 \times (-2^3) + 0 \times 2^2 + 1 \times 2^1 + 0 \times 2^0$	-6
1	0	0	1	$= 1 \times (-2^3) + 0 \times 2^2 + 0 \times 2^1 + 1 \times 2^0$	-7
1	0	0	0	$= 1 \times (-2^3) + 0 \times 2^2 + 0 \times 2^1 + 0 \times 2^0$	-8

Table 9,3: The set of all four bit signed 2's complement integers

In this case, the set of $2^4=16$ unique binary sequences is used to count from $-2^3=-8$ to $2^3-1=+7$.

Using these tables, we can report the following conclusions regarding the **Signed 2's Complement Representation**:

1. Given 'm' bits, the set of signed integers is generated by multiplying the MSB in the unsigned binary expansion by -1

2. Assuming 'm' bits, one can represent 2^m signed integers counting from a minimum value of -2^{m-1} to a maximum value of $+2^{m-1}-1$.

Binary to Decimal Conversion

Conversion from base 2 to base 10 is quite straightforward as we demonstrate in the following examples.

Applying the above table, for m=3 bits,

$$(101)_2 = -1 \times 2^2 + 0 \times 2^1 + 1 \times 2^0$$
$$= -1 \times 4 + 0 \times 2 + 1 \times 1$$
$$= (-3)_{10}$$

Assuming m=12 bits,
$(100101111001)_2$

$$= -1 \times 2^{11} + 0 \times 2^{10} + 0 \times 2^9 + 1 \times 2^8 + 0 \times 2^7$$
$$+ 1 \times 2^6 + 1 \times 2^5 + 1 \times 2^4 + 1 \times 2^3 + 0 \times 2^2 + 0 \times 2^1 + 1 \times 2^0$$
$$= -1 \times 2048 + 0 \times 1024 + 0 \times 512 + 1 \times 256 + 0 \times 128$$
$$+ 1 \times 64 + 1 \times 32 + 1 \times 16 + 1 \times 8 + 0 \times 4 + 0 \times 2 + 1 \times 1$$
$$= -2048 + 256 + 64 + 32 + 16 + 8 + 1$$
$$= (-1671)_{10}$$

Assuming m=8 bits, consider converting $(10111010)_2$ to base 10:

-2^7	2^6	2^5	2^4	2^3	2^2	2^1	2^0
-128	64	32	16	8	4	2	1
1	0	1	1	1	0	1	0

Visually, we only need to consider the columns where the bit value is one (the zero values to do not contribute to the sum); hence,

$(10111010)_2 = -128 + 32 + 16 + 8 + 2$
$$= (-70)_{10}$$

Assuming m=10 bits, consider converting $(1000000011)_2$ to base 10:

-2^9	2^8	2^7	2^6	2^5	2^4	2^3	2^2	2^1	2^0
-512	256	128	64	32	16	8	4	2	1
1	0	0	0	0	0	0	0	1	1

$(1000000011)_2 = -512 + 2 + 1$
$$= (-509)_{10}$$

Exercises:

Convert the following signed two's complement binary integers to their decimal values:

a. $(10000)_2 = (\ ?\ )_{10}$

b. $(000100)_2 = (\ ?\ )_{10}$

c. $(100001)_2 = (\ ?\ )_{10}$

d. $(10101010)_2 = (\ ?\ )_{10}$

e. $(1001011001)_2 = (\ ?\ )_{10}$

f. $(00001011)_2 = (\ ?\ )_{10}$

g. $(00010110)_2 = (\ ?\ )_{10}$

h. $(00101100)_2 = (\ ?\ )_{10}$

i. $(01011000)_2 = (\ ?\ )_{10}$

Chapter Ten: Important Observations III

The Table Pattern

It is a simple matter to generate lists of signed two's complement integers similar to the ones shown in Tables 9.1-9.3. Let's revisit the m=3 table

Binary	Decimal
011	+3
010	+2
001	+1
000	0
111	-1
110	-2
101	-3
100	-4

As with the unsigned case, the leftmost (MSB) column in the binary expansion has half the list of binary sequences starting with zero and half the list starting with one. However, as we move from left to right, in addition to halving the number of zeros and ones, the pattern that develops in the next column begins with ones at the top of the column. If you can picture this, except for the MSB column, all other columns from the unsigned pattern are effectively 'flipped' upside down. Double check and verify that this is so for the m=4 table in order to make sure this pattern makes sense to you.

Exercise:

Generate the complete table of signed 2's complement integers for the m=5 bit case using the column by column pattern. Check various values in your table to ensure that the binary values correspond to the correct decimal values.

Maximum/Minimum Values

It is extremely important to get used to recognizing certain 2's complement binary sequences containing 'm' bits. First, we already know that the minimum value expressed in decimal is always $(-2^{m-1})_{10}$ and the maximum value must be $(+(2^{m-1}-1))_{10}$. When expressed in base 2, the minimum value will always be a one followed by a string of 'm-1' zeros and the maximum value will be zero followed a string of 'm-1' ones. You can easily verify that this is the case by checking the tables generated so far for various values of 'm'.

Consider the following table whose rows show the minimum and maximum signed values assuming different numbers of bits in the representation:

m	Minimum Value in base 10	Minimum Value in base 2	Maximum Value in base 10	Maximum Value in base 2
4	$-2^3=-8$	1000	$2^3-1=+7$	0111
8	$-2^7=-128$	1000 0000	$2^8-1=+127$	0111 1111
11	$-2^{10}=-1024$	100 0000 0000	$2^{10}-1$ $=+1023$	011 1111 1111

So it should be a very, very, very straightforward exercise to determine the minimum and maximum signed values when the number of bits 'm' is specified. For example, given m=16 bits (2 bytes), we can immediately conclude that

$$+(2^{15}-1)_{10} = (+32767)_{10} = (0111\ 1111\ 1111\ 1111)_2$$
$$(-2^{15})_{10} = (-32768)_{10} = (1000\ 0000\ 0000\ 0000)_2$$

The Sign Bit

One very useful consequence of this representation is that the MSB automatically tells us the arithmetic sign of the number.

- MSB = sign of the 2's complement integer
- MSB is often referred to as the '**sign bit**'

It's pretty straightforward, but go back to the tables and convince yourself that this is the case. Observe, without knowing the actual value, we can immediately conclude that the sign of $(101010111110001)_2$ is negative and that $(011110111111011110101010101010)_2$ is nonnegative simply by inspecting the sign bit. In digital computer systems, the MSB is made available in order to indicate the sign of a number (for example, in order to execute an instruction such as 'if a value is less than zero, then go do something').

Sign Extension

Using the 2's complement tables presented for various numbers of bits, consider the following

$$m = 2: (10)_2 = (-2)_{10}$$
$$m = 3: (110)_2 = (-2)_{10}$$
$$m = 4: (1110)_2 = (-2)_{10}$$

and

$$m = 2: (01)_2 = (+1)_{10}$$
$$m = 3: (001)_2 = (+1)_{10}$$
$$m = 4: (0001)_2 = (+1)_{10}$$

Observe that, if the signed two's complement binary representation of a number is known for 'm' bits, its representation is easily ascertained if one requires more bits. _Simply 'extend' the sign bit out to the desired number of bits._

For example,

$m = 4$: $(1011)_2 = (-5)_{10}$
$m = 8$: $(1111\ 1011)_2 = (-5)_{10}$
$m = 16$: $(1111\ 1111\ 1111\ 1011)_2 = (-5)_{10}$

As another example,

$m = 4$: $(0101)_2 = (+5)_{10}$
$m = 8$: $(0000\ 0101)_2 = (+5)_{10}$
$m = 16$: $(0000\ 0000\ 0000\ 0101)_2 = (+5)_{10}$

Sign extension retains the basic properties of counting in that the table for $m = 2$ bits is contained in the table for $m = 3$ bits which is contained in the table for $m = 4$ bits and so on. Thus we are left with the desirable result that the two's complement representation remains consistent across any number of bits.

There are certain binary sequences that experts in binary numbers should automatically be able to recognize given 'm' bits (e.g. zero, one, minimum value, maximum value, powers of 2, numbers near a power of two, etc). Applying sign extension, here's another important one to add to your list:

- $(-1)_{10}$ is **_always_** an m-bit _string of ones_ when using the signed two's complement representation (go back and check the tables to see that this is so).

Example: m=16 bits ➜ $(-1)_{10} = (1111\ 1111\ 1111\ 1111)_2$

Exercises

1. Given m=12 bits, determine the maximum and minimum values that can be represented using signed 2's complement representation. Make sure to write these out in base 2 and base 10.

2. Assuming signed two's complement: $(100000000000000)_2 = (?)_{10}$

3. Assuming signed two's complement: $(10000000011)_2 = (?)_{10}$

4. Recall the oddness/evenness property introduced for unsigned binary integers. By inspecting the various m-bit tables introduced, verify that this property remains intact for the signed 2's complement representation.

5. Is $(101010111111111100010)_2$ positive or negative? Is it odd or even?

6. Is $(001010111111111100011)_2$ positive or negative? Is it odd or even?

7. Using the signed two's complement representation, the $m = 4$ bit value of $(+7)_{10} = (0111)_2$. Using sign extension, write this value as an 32-bit signed two's complement integer.

8. Using the signed two's complement representation, the $m = 5$ bit value of $(-12)_{10} = (10100)_2$. Using sign extension, write this value as an 32-bit signed two's complement integer.

9. $(111111111111111111)_2 = (?)_{10}$. Provide your answer assuming the binary number is
   a. unsigned
   b. signed 2's complement

10. For m=8 bits, compare the binary values for $(+7)_{10}$, $(+14)_{10}$, $(+28)_{10}$. Do the 'shift left/multiply by 2' and 'shift right/divide by 2' properties introduced for unsigned numbers remain intact for nonnegative integers.

11. For m=8 bits, compare the binary values for $(-1)_{10}$, $(-2)_{10}$, $(-4)_{10}$. Do the 'shift left/multiply by 2' and 'shift right/divide by 2' properties introduced for unsigned numbers remain intact for negative integers.

12. How does sign extension play a role when dividing $(-4)_{10}$ by two versus dividing $(+4)_{10}$ by two?

13. Recall the base expansion algorithm introduced to convert unsigned base 10 to unsigned base 2 using the shift right and oddness/evenness approach. Does this algorithm still work for 2's complement integers?

14. Consider a variation on the shift right and oddness/evenness approach for base 10 conversion to base 2. Instead of checking the LSB and dividing by 2, try checking the sign bit and multiplying by 2. How does the output of this approach differ from the shift right approach?

Chapter Eleven: Signed Two's Complement Binary Arithmetic:

As pointed out previously, subtraction can be interpreted as the addition of negative numbers. By extending our set of unsigned integers to signed integers, we can, without modification, retain the binary addition methodology already introduced. This approach removes the immediate need to introduce a new binary subtraction algorithm while keeping the addition operation as fundamental.

A Mathematical Note: Observe that extending our set of numbers from unsigned to signed integers is both mathematically consistent and algebraically sound. For instance, if one wants to solve for 'x' in the equation ax=b given two integers 'a' and 'b', it should be clear that the solution need not be an integer (e.g. set a=3 and b=5). Rather than introduce the explicit operation of 'division', we keep the operation of multiplication as fundamental and extend the solution set to include the rational numbers. So, instead of 'dividing' to obtain the solution, we **multiply by the reciprocal** a^{-1} (i.e. the 'multiplicative inverse') in order to characterize the solution. A deeper algebraic example is born out of attempting to solve the equation $x^2+1=0$. Under these circumstances, the set of real numbers must be extended to the set of complex numbers in order to encompass the solution set.

And, now, back to binary addition ….

Consider the following m=4 bit examples and observe that the mechanics of binary addition remain unchanged. The **_one difference to get used to_** is that the carry flag will no longer be immediately useful for contributing to the final answer as it did for the unsigned case.

(-5) + (+3) = -2 ("Addition")

```
Carry 0 1 1
        1011
      + 0011
C=0   1110  = (-2)₁₀
```
$$\text{Carry } 0\ 1\ 1$$
$$1011$$
$$+\ 0011$$
$$C=0\quad 1110\ =\ (-2)_{10}$$

(+4) + (-5) = -1 ("Subtraction")

$$\text{Carry } 0\ 0\ 0$$
$$0100$$
$$+\ 1011$$
$$C=0\quad 1111\ =\ (-1)_{10}$$

$(-2) + (+4) = +2$

$$
\begin{array}{r}
1110 \\
+\ 0100 \\
\hline
\mathbf{C=1}\ \ 0010
\end{array}
$$
$= (+2)_{10}$

$(-2) + (-4) = -6$

$$
\begin{array}{r}
1110 \\
+\ 1100 \\
\hline
\mathbf{C=1}\ \ 1010
\end{array}
$$
$= (-6)_{10}$

$(+4) + (-4) = 0$

$$
\begin{array}{r}
0100 \\
+\ 1100 \\
\hline
\mathbf{C=1}\ \ 0000
\end{array}
$$
$= (0)_{10}$

Important Conclusions:

- For the purposes of binary <u>addition (or 'subtraction')</u>, in contrast to the unsigned case, <u>the carry flag does not provide us with consistently meaningful information</u> to tell us if more bits are required for the calculation.
- The carry flag indicates when the sum of the three bits in the MSB column is greater than or equal to 2. For the purposes of understanding computer system applications beyond the scope of this introduction, it is important to be able to recognize its value based upon the mechanics of binary addition. Therefore, we will still note its value in our examples.

For unsigned binary addition, the carry flag is useful for indicating when the sum is greater than the range of represented numbers using 'm' bits. If the carry flag does not provide this information for the signed case, we must address how to determine this condition. Imagine writing a program for an m-bit computer that added two signed numbers and the actual result ended up outside the range of represented numbers. If this condition is not recognized, the results could be catastrophic. This is one major reason why we have paid such detailed attention to characterizing the maximum and minimum values given the representation.

Overflow Condition

Given 'm' bits, an <u>overflow</u> condition occurs when the sum of two signed numbers yields a result that is either greater than or less than the range of represented numbers

<u>Examples</u>:   m=4 bits → can only represent signed integers between -8 and +7

> **Consider**: $(+6) + (+3) = +9$
>
> $$\begin{array}{r} 0110 \\ +\ 0011 \\ \hline \mathbf{C=0}\ \ 1001 \ = (-7)_{10} \end{array}$$
>
> **<u>Notice</u>**: MSB=1 → Result appears negative after
adding two positive numbers!!!

> **Consider**: $(-5) + (-4) = -9$
>
> $$\begin{array}{r} 1011 \\ +\ 1100 \\ \hline \mathbf{C=1}\ \ 0111 \ = (+7)_{10} \end{array}$$
>
> **<u>Notice</u>**: MSB=0 → Result appears nonnegative
after adding two negative numbers!!!

Important Conclusions:
- Carry flag <u>cannot</u> indicate the overflow condition
- You should be able to create a few examples to convince yourself that overflow cannot occur when adding a positive number to a negative number (or vice versa).
- Overflow occurs if the operands are either <u>both</u> positive or <u>both</u> negative <u>AND</u> their sum ends up outside of the set of values that can be represented by the specified number of bits.

In the signed 2's complement representation, the overflow condition can be detected by comparing the sign bits of the operands with the sign bit of the result.

<u>Introduce an overflow flag</u>: **W**
- Set **W=1**, if, after adding
  - two nonnegative numbers (i.e. sign bit of both operands is zero), the resulting MSB=1 (i.e. the sign bit implies a negative result)
  - two negative numbers (i.e. sign bit of both operands is one), the resulting MSB=0 (i.e. the sign bit implies a nonnegative result)
- Otherwise, **W=0**

Some examples using m=8 bits (i.e. we can only represent values between -128 and +127)

$(+127) + (-128) = -1$

$$
\begin{array}{r}
0111\ 1111 \\
+\ 1000\ 0000 \\
\hline
1111\ 1111 \\
\end{array}
= (-1)_{10}
$$

C=1, W=0

$(+127) + (-127) = 0$

$$
\begin{array}{r}
0111\ 1111 \\
+\ 1000\ 0001 \\
\hline
0000\ 0000 \\
\end{array}
= (0)_{10}
$$

C=1, W=0

$(-128) + (-128) = -256$

$$
\begin{array}{r}
1000\ 0000 \\
+\ 1000\ 0000 \\
\hline
0000\ 0000 \\
\end{array}
= (0)_{10} \quad \text{(Overflow occurred)}
$$

C=1, W=1

$(+127) + (+4) = +131$

$$
\begin{array}{r}
0111\ 1111 \\
+\ 0000\ 0100 \\
\hline
1000\ 0011 \\
\end{array}
= (-125)_{10} \quad \text{(Overflow occurred)}
$$

C=0, W=1

Important note regarding Hexadecimal notation

We do not use nor have we introduced 'signed hexadecimal numbers'. With two's complement representation, we still use the same four bit binary patterns in the form of hexadecimal digits in order to shorten the length of the number.

Consider the preceding examples when written using Hexadecimal shorthand:

$$7F + 80 = FF \quad \text{and } \mathbf{C=0, W=0}$$
$$7F + 81 = 00 \quad \text{and } \mathbf{C=1, W=0}$$
$$80 + 80 = 00 \quad \text{and } \mathbf{C=1, W=1}$$
$$7F + 04 = 83 \quad \text{and } \mathbf{C=0, W=1}$$

Arithmetic Negation

It is often useful to be able to convert a positive number to a negative one or vice versa (for example, almost every calculator in the known universe has a +/- button). Whereas a computer systems person would call this process **'arithmetic negation'**, a mathematician might use the phrase 'computing the additive inverse' (where an *additive inverse* is something you add to any number to get zero).

An advantageous consequence of the 2's complement representation is that the process of arithmetic negation is quite straightforward. Before explaining how to do this, we must introduce a definition

The Logical Complement

The *bitwise* **'Logical Complement'** (also known as the **'Logical NOT'** or 'Logical Negation') of a binary number is constructed bitwise by changing all zeros to ones and all ones to zeros. We will denote this operation by using the word '**NOT**'.

For example,
- NOT(1001 0011) = 0110 1100
- NOT(1111 0001 0101) = 0000 1110 1010

To compute the additive inverse of (i.e. to arithmetically negate) a signed two's complement binary number:
1. **First, take the *bitwise logical complement* of the binary number**
2. **Then, *add one* to the result**

Let's consider some examples for m=4 bits:

We know that $(+5)_{10} = (0101)_2$. The signed two's complement binary representation of $(-5)_{10}$ can be found as follows:
1. (Take the logical complement) NOT(0101) = 1010
2. (Add one) $(1010)_2 + (0001)_2 = (1011)_2 = (-5)_{10}$

This recipe works both ways. Starting with $(-5)_{10} = (1011)_2$, the signed two's complement binary representation of $(+5)_{10}$ can be found as follows:
1. (Take the logical complement) NOT(1011) = 0100
2. (Add one) $(0100)_2 + (0001)_2 = (0101)_2 = (+5)_{10}$

One more, just to be sure, $(-2)_{10} = (1110)_2$. The signed two's complement binary representation of $(+2)_{10}$ can be found as follows:

1. (Take the logical complement) NOT(1110) = 0001
2. (Add one) $(0001)_2 + (0001)_2 = (0010)_2 = (+2)_{10}$

Exercises:

1. Assuming signed two's complement representation using m=8 bits, add the following numbers **using binary addition** AND determine the values of the C and W flags in response to each calculation.

   a. $(-128)_{10} + (+100)_{10}$

   b. $(+5)_{10} + (+7)_{10}$

   c. $(+5)_{10} + (-7)_{10}$

   d. $(-5)_{10} + (+7)_{10}$

   e. $(-5)_{10} + (-7)_{10}$

   f. $(+120) + (+100)$

   g. $(-120) + (-100)$

   h. $(6A)_{16} + (E2)_{16}$

   i. $(A7)_{16} + (35)_{16}$

   j. $(80)_{16} + (80)_{16}$

2. ***Computing additive inverses***: Apply the 'take complement and add one' algorithm to arithmetically negate the given values

   a. Convert $(-3)_{10} = (1101)_2$ to $(+3)_{10}$.

   b. Convert $(-1)_{10} = (1111)2$ to $(+1)10$.

   c. Apply this algorithm to $(-8)_{10} = (1000)_2$. Pay close attention to the fact that, in this representation, *the most negative integer will not have an additive inverse*. Go back and check the tables to make sure that you see that this is so.

   d. Apply this algorithm to $(0)_{10} = (0000)_2$.

e. Express $(-14)_{10}$ in signed two's complement representation using m = 16 bits according to the following steps:

    1. First, express $(+14)_{10}$ using m=5 bits

    2. Apply the 'take complement and add one' algorithm

    3. Use sign extension to extend your answer out to m=16 bits

Chapter Twelve: Bitwise Logical Operations

Now that we have had a chance to introduce arithmetic operations using binary numbers, we now shift gears to discuss logical operations. The operations introduced here should be a review of material contained within a typical introductory programming course. In addition, they are also referred to in other areas such as discrete structures, Boolean algebra, computer architecture and introductory philosophy courses on logic. The term '*bitwise*' simply refers to the fact that the operations introduced in this section are performed independently on each bit contained within a binary sequence.

Bitwise logical NOT
For the sake of completeness, we restate that the 'Logical Complement' or the 'Logical NOT' of a binary number is constructed by changing all zeros to ones and all ones to zeros. When given a set of bits, this operation is performed 'bitwise' (i.e. independently on each bit).

For example,
- NOT(1001 0011) = 0110 1100
- NOT(1111 0001 0101) = 0000 1110 1010

Bitwise logical OR

a	b		a OR b
0	0		0
0	1		1
1	0		1
1	1		1

Table 12.1: Truth table defining the logical OR between two bits

In Boolean algebra, it is often the convention to equate the bit value '1' with a logical TRUE and the bit value '0' with a logical FALSE. Applying this convention, we can intuitively summarize the above table by noting that the OR between two bits can only be FALSE when BOTH 'a' and 'b' are FALSE. If either one or both of 'a' or 'b' are TRUE, then 'a OR b' must be TRUE.

Let's consider some examples to make sure we are comfortable with performing this operation bitwise (i.e. *column-by-column*).

```
        1000 0000
OR      0111 1111
        1111 1111
```

```
        0000 0001
OR   0001 1111
        0001 1111
```

The above examples can also be expressed in hexadecimal:
- 80 OR 7F = FF
- 01 OR 1F = 1F

Many high level programming languages have bitwise logical operations that can be performed on integers. If the bits in the above examples are interpreted as signed two's complement binary numbers, the above examples can be written as:
- -128 OR 127 = ☐1
- 1 OR 31 = 31

Bitwise logical AND

a	b		a AND b
0	0		0
0	1		0
1	0		0
1	1		1

Table 12.2: Truth table defining the logical AND between two bits

Again, equating the bit value '1' with a logical TRUE and the bit value '0' with a logical FALSE, intuitively, we see that the AND between two bits can only be TRUE when BOTH 'a' and 'b' are TRUE.

Some examples,

```
     1000 0000
AND  0111 1111
     0000 0000
```

```
     0000 0001
AND  0001 1111
     0000 0001
```

The above examples can also be expressed in hexadecimal:
- 80 AND 7F = 00
- 01 AND 1F = 01

Or, as signed 2's complement integers
- -128 AND 127 = 0
- 1 AND 31 = 1

Bitwise logical Exclusive OR (XOR)

While the XOR operation is not considered 'fundamental' from a Boolean algebra perspective (it is derivable from the NOT, OR and AND operations), it is so pervasive and logically important that no discussion could be considered complete without it.

a	b		a XOR b
0	0		0
0	1		1
1	0		1
1	1		0

Table 12.3: Truth table defining the logical XOR between two bits

Intuitively, we see that the XOR between two bits can only be TRUE when either 'a' or 'b' are exclusively TRUE, but not both.

Some examples,

```
      1000 0000
XOR   0111 1111
      1111 1111
```

```
      0000 0001
XOR   0001 1111
      0001 1110
```

The above examples can also be expressed in hexadecimal:

- 80 XOR 7F = FF
- 01 XOR 1F = 1E

Or, as signed 2's complement integers

- -128 XOR 127 = -1
- 1 XOR 31 = 30

Revisiting Binary Addition

a	b		Carry	Sum
0	0		0	0
0	1		0	1
1	0		0	1
1	1		1	0

Table 12.4: Binary Addition Table for the 'Half Adder'

With the above logical operations defined, we now revisit the binary addition operation on two bits. Please compare the sum and carry operations with the logical AND, and the logical XOR operations. The key point to be raised is that digital computers do not 'arithmetically compute' addition. Instead, digital circuitry is only capable of performing logical operations such as NOT, OR, AND, etc. Therefore, digital circuits **_simulate_** arithmetic addition of two bits via the logical AND and logical XOR operations. Such a digital circuit is often referred to as a 'half adder'. The so-called 'full adder' which performs three bit addition by taking into account the Carry In is also easily implemented using the NOT, OR, AND and XOR operations (this is a topic often reserved for Boolean algebra and digital circuit design).

Inverted Logic

It is also possible to define the logical complement of the of above operations

$$NOR = NOT(OR)$$
$$NAND = NOT(AND)$$
$$XNOR = NOT(XOR)$$

Such operations are sometimes referred to as inverted logical operations and are derivable from the above tables simply by taking their logical complement.

a	b		a NOR b	a NAND b	a XNOR b
0	0		1	1	1
0	1		0	1	0
1	0		0	1	0
1	1		0	0	1

Table 12.5: Inverted Logic

These operations are also important when it comes to efficiently describing Boolean algebra as well as considering practical applications to digital circuit design.

Exercises

Perform the following bitwise logical operations

1. $NOT((1EAE)_{16})$
2. $(1EAE)_{16}$ XOR $(FFFF)_{16}$
3. $(1EAE)_{16}$ OR $(1EAE)_{16}$
4. $(1EAE)_{16}$ AND $NOT((1EAE)_{16})$
5. $(1EAE)_{16}$ OR $NOT((1EAE)_{16})$
6. $(1EAE)_{16}$ AND $(0002)_{16}$
7. $(1EAE)_{16}$ OR $(0001)_{16}$

8. Given an m-bit binary integer, 'Z', explain how performing the following consecutive set of operations determines oddness/evenness of Z:
   a. Compute: Z AND 1
   b. If result=0, then Z is even

9. Given any 16-bit binary integer, 'Z', explain how performing the following consecutive set of operations determines the sign of Z:
   a. Compute: Z AND -32768
   b. If result=1, then Z is negative

10. (Using the OR operation to set a bit to a value of one) Given any 16-bit binary integer, 'Z', explain the value of the MSB of Z after the following operation is performed

    Compute: Z OR -32768

    What will be the effect of this operation on the MSB versus the other 15-bits of Z?

11. (Using the AND operation to reset a bit to a value of zero) Given any 16-bit binary integer, 'Z', explain the value of the MSB of Z after the following operation is performed

Compute: Z AND 32767

What will be the effect of this operation on the MSB versus the other 15-bits of Z?

12. (Using the AND operation to reset a bit to a value zero) Given any 16-bit binary integer, 'Z', explain the value of the LSB of Z after the following operation is performed

Compute: Z AND -2

What will be the effect of this operation on the other 15-bits of Z?

Printed in Great Britain
by Amazon

11358900R00062